WORK IN THE
MUSIC INDUSTRY

by Marty Erickson

BrightP◇int Press

San Diego, CA

BrightP◆int Press

© 2020 BrightPoint Press
an imprint of ReferencePoint Press, Inc.
Printed in the United States

For more information, contact:
BrightPoint Press
PO Box 27779
San Diego, CA 92198
www.BrightPointPress.com

LIBRARY OF CONGRESS CATALOGING-IN-PUBLICATION DATA

Names: Erickson, Marty, 1991- author.
Title: Work in the music industry / by Marty Erickson.
Description: San Diego, CA : ReferencePoint Press, [2020] | Series: Career
    finder | Audience: Grade 9 to 12. | Includes index.
Identifiers: LCCN 2019005399 (print) | LCCN 2019007800 (ebook) | ISBN
    9781682827321 (ebook) | ISBN 9781682827314 (hardcover)
Subjects: LCSH: Music trade--Vocational guidance--Juvenile literature.
Classification: LCC ML3795 (ebook) | LCC ML3795 .E77 2020 (print) | DDC
    780.23--dc23
LC record available at https://lccn.loc.gov/2019005399

CONTENTS

THE MUSIC INDUSTRY

Musicians and Singers

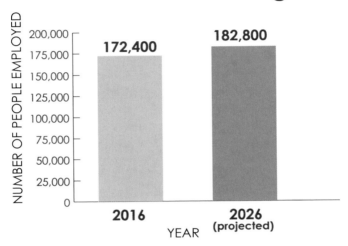

Sound Engineers

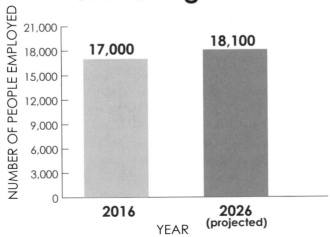

Popular Types of Music in 2018
(Based on Number of Albums Streamed)

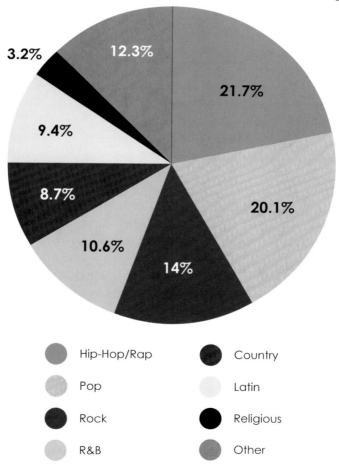

3.2% 12.3% 21.7% 9.4% 8.7% 10.6% 14% 20.1%

Hip-Hop/Rap   Country

Pop   Latin

Rock   Religious

R&B   Other

WHAT IS THE MUSIC INDUSTRY?

Fans crowd around a stage. They are in a concert hall. They have come to hear a band. They cheer as the musicians take the stage. Bright lights shine on the band. One musician is a drummer. She keeps a steady beat. Another plays the piano. A third musician is a singer. He also

At live concerts, musicians perform songs they have developed and practiced.

plays a guitar. His voice carries through a

microphone. The audience knows the lyrics.

Some people sing along. Others dance to

the music. The audience claps and cheers

as the song ends. The band waves to the crowd and smiles.

Musicians are just one part of the music industry. They need the help of many people to become successful. Audio technicians set up sound equipment at concerts. This includes microphones. Lighting technicians control the lighting at concerts. They create light shows and special effects.

Live performances are just one part of a musician's job. A musician's job begins with songwriting. Some musicians do not write their own songs. They hire songwriters.

Lighting technicians install and operate lighting equipment for concerts.

Songwriters often spend many hours composing a song's lyrics and melody. Songwriters work with **record** producers. Record producers help create recordings of songs. A songwriter plays a song for a record producer. If the producer

Sound engineers use special equipment to change or improve the sound of a song.

likes it, she finds a singer or band to record

the song.

Musicians record songs in studios.

They work with record producers. Record

producers give musicians feedback. They work with sound engineers. Sound engineers piece different parts of the recordings together into one song. They make sure the sound quality is good. Sometimes they add sound effects.

The music industry is competitive. It takes a lot of patience and determination to become successful. But there are many types of jobs available. People who work in the industry are creative and persistent. They do not give up on their dreams.

CHAPTER ONE

MUSICIAN

There would not be a music industry without musicians. Musicians sing and play instruments. Some write their own songs. They work long hours. Some musicians go on concert tours around the world. Others perform on a smaller scale.

WHAT THEY DO

Musicians must be willing to work for little money when they begin their careers. Many

MINIMUM EDUCATION: A college degree is not required. Voice or instrument lessons can help musicians develop skills.

PERSONAL QUALITIES: Patient, dedicated, creative, hardworking

CERTIFICATION AND LICENSING: None

WORKING CONDITIONS: Musicians often work long hours. They have to travel when they go on tours.

SALARY: The average pay for musicians in 2017 was $26.96 per hour.

NUMBER OF JOBS: 172,400 in 2016

FUTURE JOB OUTLOOK: The number of jobs is expected to grow 6% from 2016 to 2026, or an additional 10,400 jobs.

venues do not pay very much. Sometimes they do not pay musicians at all. Musicians may have to take a full-time job in addition to working on their music. A second job helps them make a living.

Many musicians are part of a band.

Musicians need to build connections.

Meeting people in the industry is important.

Some record producers go to shows to

see musicians perform. They may decide

to work with a musician if they like the

performance. It is important for musicians to

seek out and take new opportunities. This can help them become successful.

Some musicians make records. They work with record producers. People can buy their records. This helps musicians make a living. It can also help make their music more widely popular.

Musicians record songs in recording studios. A band first records the background music. The singer tries different ways of performing a song with the background music. The record producer and the singer work together to try new styles. They may try a different section in the middle. They may lengthen or shorten the introduction. There can be a lot of trial and error in the process.

The record producer stands on one side of a soundproof room behind a thick wall of glass. The singer can still see the producer. The singer wears headphones. This allows him to hear the background music. It also lets him hear the producer's feedback. A microphone records his vocals. The singer may spend many hours in the studio. It can take several days of recording to produce one song. Putting an **album** together can take months. That does not

Recording studios are soundproof. This prevents any outside noises from being recorded.

include the time needed to write the songs

or rehearse them.

   After an album is released, some

musicians go on tour. Tours can last for

more than a year. Musicians play in many

Some musicians perform in parades.

cities in a short period of time. They

promote their music.

Not all musicians are lead singers.

Many different musicians work together to

create a song. Instrumentalists create the

background music. They play many different instruments, such as drums and the piano. Some bands do not have a singer. Their albums are only instrumental music. Bands specialize in different **genres**, such as classical or rock. For example, 12 Ensemble is a classical music group. It is made up of twelve musicians. Each musician plays a stringed instrument. They do not have a director. Sometimes rehearsals can be difficult. But the group says, "Everyone chips in with different ideas and it works." The ability to work well with others is important for any musician.

Some musicians perform in orchestras. Many different instruments make up an orchestra. Orchestra musicians play classical music. They perform in concerts. A conductor directs the musicians. She makes sure they play together. Orchestras may perform around the world.

Many musicians have social media accounts. Social media helps them connect with fans and build a following. Musicians also use social media to share their music. Some post videos of their performances on YouTube. This platform is especially helpful for new musicians. Some musicians have

Orchestras vary in size. Chamber orchestras have fewer than fifty musicians.

become well-known after sharing their

videos on YouTube.

Some musicians never sign with

a record label. They are able to be

independent. They travel locally. They perform at small concert venues. They record and mix their own albums. Many independent musicians rely on social media to sell their albums.

TRAINING

Some musicians are self-taught. They build their skills on their own. Others have vocal coaches. Coaches help singers practice and prepare. It is possible to sing incorrectly. This can damage a singer's voice. When singers perform a lot, their vocal cords may get tired. Vocal cords are a part of the throat that helps

Singer-songwriter Charlie Puth became successful after a YouTube video he made went viral.

produce sounds. Singers can get vocal cord injuries. Lessons can help. Vocal coaches teach singers how to perform without hurting themselves.

Some musicians take lessons to learn how to play different instruments. It is useful to be able to play more than one instrument. Lessons help musicians improve their skills.

LOOKING AHEAD

Musicians are dedicated to their craft. They do not give up. People work hard to make a living as musicians. But the job can be rewarding. Musicians enjoy the work they do. They like being creative. People around the world listen to music every day. Musicians entertain many people.

FIND OUT MORE

Atlantic Records
website: www.atlanticrecords.com/posts/
category/how-get-signed

Atlantic Records is a well-known record label.
It has been in business for more than seventy
years. Its website gives helpful information
about the music industry, such as how
musicians can sign with a label.

Berklee Career Communities
website: www.berklee.edu/careers

Berklee Career Communities is a site run by
Berklee College of Music. It gives information
about different careers in the music industry.

Bureau of Labor Statistics (BLS)
website: www.bls.gov/careeroutlook/2015/
article/careers-for-music-lovers.htm

The BLS gives information about different
career options, including music industry
careers. It reports on job requirements
and growth.

CHAPTER TWO

SONGWRITER

Songwriters have an important role in the music industry. They write song lyrics and melodies. They create the songs that play on the radio. They also write the songs people listen to in concerts. Some musicians are songwriters. They perform the songs they write. Other songwriters are not musicians. They write music for musicians.

MINIMUM EDUCATION: A college degree is not needed. It is helpful to know the basics of songwriting and music theory.

PERSONAL QUALITIES: Hardworking, creative, a good writer

CERTIFICATION AND LICENSING: None

WORKING CONDITIONS: Songwriters often work long hours. Many work from home.

SALARY: The average 2017 salary was $50,590 per year, or $24.32 per hour.

NUMBER OF JOBS: 74,800 in 2016

FUTURE JOB OUTLOOK: The number of jobs is expected to grow 6% from 2016 to 2026, or an additional 4,300 jobs.

WHAT THEY DO

Becoming a songwriter is difficult.

Songwriting is a competitive field. Many

songwriters have to find a second job to

help support themselves. It can be hard

Many songwriters first write their lyrics in notebooks.

to find a record producer who is willing to

listen to a new songwriter's work.

Many songwriters work from home.

They experiment with different lyrics and

melodies. They come up with original song

ideas. Songwriters may have different

processes. Some start with the lyrics. Then they add the melody. Some have an idea for a melody. They come up with the lyrics later. Others may come up with the melody and lyrics at the same time.

Songwriters get inspiration from many sources. Courtney Barnett is a songwriter. She says, "If I'm writing and I get stuck on a word, I might look up and see a billboard with a word I like. Or I might see a couple having an argument." Barnett guesses what the couple may be arguing about. This can spark an idea.

When a song is ready, songwriters share it with record producers. Record producers decide whether to record the song. If they like the song, producers find musicians to perform it. If the songwriter is also a musician, she could perform her own song. The song is recorded in a studio.

Songwriters get paid about nine cents each time someone buys their song. They get paid different rates each time their song is played on the radio or through a streaming service. Spotify is an example of a popular streaming service. The payments songwriters receive are called **royalties**.

Musicians who are part of a band may work together to write songs.

Many people have to buy or play songs in order for songwriters to make enough money to live on.

TRAINING

Songwriters do not need a college degree to be successful. But they do need to have

Listening to other music can help inspire songwriters.

a broad knowledge of music. They study

music on the radio. They notice patterns.

Popular songs often have similarities. They

may have similar rhythms or instruments.

Songwriters need to know what makes

a hit.

People can take songwriting classes. These classes help them learn how to write songs. Music theory classes can also be helpful. Music theory is the study of melodies and music. It helps people learn how to read and write music. Learning how to read music is similar to learning a new language. Music has rules and concepts that songwriters need to understand.

Many songwriters are musicians. They know how to play musical instruments. They can test out their songs themselves. Songwriters can also use computer songwriting programs. These programs allow writers to compose parts for different instruments. The programs record and play back the music. Songwriters can make changes as they create the song. Some songwriting programs are available as phone apps. Songwriters may spend many hours working on small sections of a song. They make sure the sections fit within the overall song.

LOOKING AHEAD

Songwriters will always be needed in the music industry. The field is not growing very quickly. But for a determined writer, it is possible to get a full-time job writing songs.

Many songwriters are also musicians. They may perform their own music.

Many songwriters do not get a lot of recognition for their work. The musicians who perform their songs may become well-known. Songwriters work behind the scenes to create music that audiences will enjoy. They do not write for the fame. They do it because songwriting is their passion. Still, some awards shows recognize songwriters. These include the Grammy Awards and the Academy Awards. A Song of the Year award is given out at the Grammys. People in the music industry vote on the best song each year. The award is given to the songwriter who wrote the song. The Academy Awards has a category for songwriters. It is called Best Original Song. This award recognizes a song written for a movie.

FIND OUT MORE

The American Society of Composers, Authors, and Publishers (ASCAP)

website: www.ascap.com

The ASCAP is an organization of more than 690,000 songwriters and other music industry professionals. It helps professionals with music copyright issues.

AmericanSongwriter.com

website: https://americansongwriter.com

This website provides daily music industry news. It also has resources and interviews with music industry professionals.

SongU

website: www.songu.com

SongU offers online songwriting classes. Teachers provide feedback and mentoring. Songwriters also can send songs to record producers.

CHAPTER THREE

RECORD PRODUCER

Record producers work with many different people. They help create music recordings. They oversee each step in the recording process. They have a clear idea of how the song should sound. They direct a team of people to help create this sound. They explain their vision to other people on the team.

MINIMUM EDUCATION: A college degree is not required, but classes can be helpful.

PERSONAL QUALITIES: Patient, hardworking, confident, able to work well with others

CERTIFICATION AND LICENSING: None

WORKING CONDITIONS: Record producers often work long hours and have tight deadlines. They mainly work in recording studios.

SALARY: The average 2017 salary was $81,520 per year, or $39.19 per hour.

NUMBER OF JOBS: 1,410 in 2017

FUTURE JOB OUTLOOK: The number of jobs is expected to grow about 12% from 2016 to 2026, or an additional 169 jobs.

WHAT THEY DO

Record producers work for record labels.

They oversee many people. They work with

musicians and songwriters in recording

studios. They also work with audio and

Record producers work with musicians in recording studios.

sound engineers. Audio engineers set

up the recording equipment. Sound

engineers edit the song. Producers give the

engineers feedback. This helps shape the

final product.

A lot of work goes into creating an album or a song. The people who work in a recording studio are a team. Record producers respect the work their coworkers do. It is important that everyone enjoys coming to work. They need to know their skills are valued. It is the producer's job to create that environment.

Steve Levine is a record producer. He started out as a sound engineer. But he does not think that background is required to become a producer. He says that producers "have to listen to a band, understand what they want, and have the patience to allow them to experiment."

Record producers supervise musicians in a recording studio. They give musicians ideas about how to perform the music. They provide feedback to help musicians improve a song. They may work with a musician to change the lyrics or the melody.

In a recording session, musicians may try many versions of a song. They may get frustrated. Record producers help encourage them. Producers build up a musician's confidence. Levine says, "They [producers] create an atmosphere where

Record producers give sound engineers feedback to help shape the overall sound of a song.

the band is open to trying new ideas."

Producers want a song to be the best it can be. This takes patience and dedication.

Record producers often use digital programs to help create recordings.

Record producers need to know how to use special programs and equipment.

These programs let them change parts of a recording. Producers work with sound engineers to make these changes.

TRAINING

Classes and training are not required to become a record producer. But they can help producers succeed. Producers need to know how to use digital programs. Some people learn these skills through online tutorials. These videos give people step-by-step instructions. People can also take classes to learn how to use these tools. They might go to college. They can get a degree in music production. Classes provide access to digital programs. They teach people how to use these programs. Classes also help students meet people in the music industry. These connections can help students build a career as a record producer.

Many record producers say that developing industry connections is more important than knowing the technology. Some producers started in entry-level jobs within the music industry. They worked as assistants in recording studios. Their job was to bring coffee and water to people. They gained experience and worked their way up. They learned new skills. They learned how to use digital programs. Then they were promoted to higher-level jobs. Eventually they became record producers. It is rare for someone to become a producer without first working in entry-level jobs.

Some people have many roles in the music industry. Jay-Z is a rapper, songwriter, and record producer.

LOOKING AHEAD

There are not many job openings for record producers. It requires hard work to become a producer. People need to be willing to start in entry-level jobs and work

Record producers work with many different people to create a record or album.

their way up. Anyone who has a passion

for music can become a producer. But it

takes time and effort. Successful producers

are patient. They persevere in the face of

obstacles. They go above and beyond

what is expected of them. They prove to

the people they work with that they are

responsible and trustworthy.

FIND OUT MORE

CareersinMusic.com

website: www.careersinmusic.com/
record-producer

CareersinMusic.com is a website that gives
information about careers in the music
industry. This includes information about the
skills and training needed for different careers.

The Music Producers Guild (MPG)

website: https://mpg.org.uk

The MPG is a group of record producers,
sound engineers, and other people in the
music industry. The MPG connects record
producers from all around the world.

CHAPTER FOUR

RADIO DJ

Radio DJs broadcast music over the radio. Stations often specialize in certain music. Some play country. Others play rock or rap. DJs introduce listeners to new music. They help songs become popular.

WHAT THEY DO

DJs are announcers for radio stations.

They play music and talk between songs.

MINIMUM EDUCATION: **A college degree is not required, but it can be helpful.**

PERSONAL QUALITIES: **Outgoing, an entertainer, a music enthusiast**

CERTIFICATION AND LICENSING: **None**

WORKING CONDITIONS: **DJs work for radio stations. They may have to work late at night or very early in the morning.**

SALARY: **The average 2017 salary was $45,180 per year, or $21.72 per hour.**

NUMBER OF JOBS: **25,050 in 2017**

FUTURE JOB OUTLOOK: **The number of jobs is expected to decline by 9% from 2016 to 2026.**

They try to sound friendly, as if they are having a conversation with their listeners. They sometimes give advice. They also share news stories. DJs research news topics. They interview people, such as listeners or musicians. They also share

Radio DJs must be confident speakers.

news about upcoming concerts. Each

radio show has a schedule. DJs stick to

the schedule. They make sure the show

runs smoothly.

DJs work with others at a radio station. They help production managers pick out songs to play. They clean the studio space. Stations usually have more than one DJ. The DJs may work together. They may cohost radio shows.

Many radio DJs are well-known within their communities. They make public appearances. They attend music festivals. They host giveaways at local venues, such as restaurants and fairs. They may give away prizes such as movie tickets. Sometimes the giveaways are bigger. They may be free vacations. DJs are outgoing. They enjoy entertaining audiences.

Many radio DJs use social media. Radio stations also have websites. DJs help update these sites. They write posts about news stories or other events. They invite fans to interact with them on these sites. DJs are always making connections with people.

TRAINING

People who want to become DJs can start developing their skills in high school. They can take public speaking and English classes. Some high schools offer classes

Radio DJs may have booths at fairs or festivals to advertise their radio station.

on radio broadcasting. Students can

practice making **playlists**. They can also

volunteer or get a part-time job at a local

Some colleges have radio stations. People can gain DJ experience by working at these stations.

radio station. This experience can help

students learn how stations work.

Aspiring DJs do not need a college

degree. But some degree programs can

be helpful. Many programs are available

for people who want to work in radio.

Students can get a two-year degree in radio broadcasting. This option focuses on developing skills to become a radio DJ. Other students may pursue a four-year degree in broadcast communication. This is a broader focus. This degree option teaches news broadcasting skills. Both types of programs focus on speaking clearly. They also offer classes on writing scripts for radio. Degree programs give students an introduction to a variety of radio formats.

Radio DJ Brandi Garcia works in San Antonio, Texas. She thinks classes can be helpful. She says, "Take a speech class.

It helped me tremendously when I was in college." Radio DJs spend a lot of time talking. They need to be comfortable telling stories and reporting news.

Some radio DJs start out in entry-level jobs at a radio station. This helps them gain experience. They learn how a radio station is run. If they work hard, they may get more responsibilities. Garcia thinks this is a good way to gain experience. She says, "Just get your foot in the door. . . . Get an **internship** or start working part-time at any station you can." Interns may fill in for DJs who are sick

Radio DJs often host and chat with guests.

or on vacation. These opportunities might

lead to a full-time position as a radio DJ.

LOOKING AHEAD

Broadcast radio has been around for

about one hundred years. Fewer young

Radio DJs help promote music.

people own radios today than in previous generations. But millions of people still listen to the radio each day. Radio DJs provide a popular form of entertainment. They help educate people about music.

FIND OUT MORE

Learn.org

website: https://learn.org/articles/Which_
Schools_Offer_Training_to_Become_a_Radio_
DJ.html

Learn.org provides academic and career
resources. It helps people find education and
employment opportunities.

**The National Association of Broadcasters
(NAB)**

website: www.nabonlineresourceguide.org

The NAB provides resources for radio DJs.
It also gives information about different
careers in broadcasting.

CHAPTER FIVE

MUSIC THERAPIST

A music therapist is a type of occupational therapist. Occupational therapists serve people who need help with daily activities. This includes people who have **disorders** or disabilities. Music therapists have musical skills. They play instruments. They may also sing. They use music to help clients. Music helps people in many ways.

MINIMUM EDUCATION: Bachelor's degree

PERSONAL QUALITIES: Compassionate, patient, a good leader, a good listener, a skilled musician

CERTIFICATION AND LICENSING: Certification through the Certification Board for Music Therapists is required to become a music therapist.

WORKING CONDITIONS: Music therapists work with people who have physical or mental disabilities. Many work in clients' homes. Others work in hospitals, nursing homes, or schools.

SALARY: The average 2017 salary was $47,680 per year, or $22.92 per hour.

NUMBER OF JOBS: 19,200 in 2016

FUTURE JOB OUTLOOK: The number of jobs is expected to grow 7% from 2016 to 2026, or an additional 1,300 jobs.

WHAT THEY DO

Music therapy is used to treat many

different people. Elizabeth Huss is a music

therapist. She works with clients who

Music therapists use music to help treat clients.

have autism. Autism is a disorder. People

with autism have difficulty communicating.

They can learn how to communicate

through music. Huss also works in a

nursing home with elderly people. Different

clients have different needs. She says,

"I have autistic [clients] that are very set in their routines. If you interrupt their routines, they go into a tantrum. So with them, I work on gently altering the routine. I do different music each week."

Some music therapists work at addiction centers. These centers help people overcome addictions. This includes drug addictions. These people may feel depressed or anxious. Music can help ease these feelings. Therapists and clients play instruments together. Playing and listening to music can calm people.

Studies show that music can improve people's moods. It can make people feel happy or relaxed. Music also helps people express their feelings. People with learning or speech disabilities may have difficulty communicating. Music therapists teach them how to express themselves through music. This can lead to new ways of coping with stress.

Music therapy also involves movement. Elderly people and people with disabilities may struggle with movement. Movement in music therapy may include strumming a guitar or beating a drum. This exercises a

Music therapy can be used to treat a variety of people, including some people who have cerebral palsy. Cerebral palsy is a developmental disorder.

person's muscles. It can improve a person's

physical abilities and coordination.

Music therapists must be in touch with

people in their clients' lives. Many music

Some music therapists work with children in schools.

therapists work with children. They talk with

the child's parents and teachers. The child's

doctor also consults with the therapist.

Sometimes they all work together to create

a therapy plan. The doctor explains goals

and treatment plans. Each client has different goals and needs.

Music therapists usually work full time. Most work forty hours each week. Sometimes they might have to work on evenings or weekends.

Music therapists work in many different environments. Some work with students in schools. Others work in hospitals or nursing homes. Some clients live in group homes. Group homes treat people who have disabilities. Therapists also often see a client in the client's home. This helps the client feel comfortable. Therapists may have an office. They keep their clients' records there. They protect their clients' privacy. They do not share information about their clients with other people.

TRAINING

Music therapists need to have a bachelor's degree. Some colleges offer degrees in music therapy. Others have broader occupational therapy degrees. Both of these degrees can help someone become a music therapist. These programs teach students music therapy techniques, such as drum circles. Students may practice these techniques with their classmates.

Drums are common instruments used in music therapy.

Certification is also needed to become a music therapist. The Certification Board for Music Therapists offers certification. Certification gives someone a license to practice music therapy. Certification requires 480 hours of supervised practice.

This means that a licensed therapist goes with the person to appointments. Licensed therapists answer questions and provide guidance. After the supervision process is done, people take a test. They become certified music therapists if they pass the test.

LOOKING AHEAD

Music therapists are in high demand. Music offers a different kind of care than typical medical care. Many medical professionals recognize music therapy's benefits. Some doctors prescribe music therapy as a treatment.

FIND OUT MORE

The American Music Therapy Association (AMTA)

website: www.musictherapy.org

The AMTA is an organization for music therapists in the United States. It gives information about education and training opportunities. It also educates the public about the benefits of music therapy.

Careers in Psychology

website: https://careersinpsychology.org

Careers in Psychology offers information about careers in the field of psychology. It also shares educational options for people pursuing these careers.

A MUSICIAN

Emilie Judge-Becker is a violin teacher. She is also a singer and violinist in a band called SlovCzech. SlovCzech is an Eastern European folk-rock band.

WHY DID YOU BECOME A MUSICIAN?

I became a musician because I love performing. I had been involved in the arts from a young age as a ballerina, actor, and singer, but for some reason violin is the one that stuck. I play with a few bands now . . . and there is something a bit magical about getting on a stage with some of your best friends, playing as loud and fast as you can, and looking past the lights to see people enjoying it with you.

CAN YOU DESCRIBE YOUR TYPICAL WORK DAY?

One of the very nice things about being a professional musician is that you often don't have to wake up early. The workday starts when kids get out of school around 3:00 p.m., and we meet them for private lessons. Private lessons are one-on-one and allow the teacher to get to know the student's musical and learning style in detail. . . . I usually teach beginner students because, for me, their quick progress and diverse ways of learning are the most interesting to observe. . . . In the evening, students go home, and musicians can meet up for practices of their own. The bands that I play with usually rehearse after dinner time. . . . Rehearsals can last anywhere from two to five hours.

WHAT DO YOU LIKE MOST ABOUT YOUR JOB?

I love the [many] people one meets as a musician. The music community is vast but has lots of small "neighborhoods." I love traveling between them. As professional musicians, we tend to be very specialized in our musical styles. I mostly play rock and klezmer [a type of traditional Eastern European Jewish music] these days. But I have friends who only play jazz, or classical, or folk. . . . Though the styles and the genres we specialize in are very different, we speak a similar language. . . . We can share fun stories from tours or rehearsals and even try to learn new techniques from each other.

WHAT ADVICE DO YOU HAVE FOR STUDENTS WHO ARE INTERESTED IN THIS CAREER?

I recommend putting in your time in the practice room . . . but also make sure to gain other skills. Mastering basic social skills like how to maintain friendships and knowing how to share [the spotlight] . . . will make you a more popular musician and a more well-rounded person. . . . Also, go to as many concerts in as many different musical styles as you can. See what you can learn from watching real pros, and find out what kind of music inspires you the most.

OTHER JOBS IN THE MUSIC INDUSTRY

- Agent

- Audio Engineer

- Band Director

- Composer

- Concert Promoter

- Manager

- Music Director

- Music Editor

- Music Journalist

- Music Librarian

- Music Supervisor

- Music Teacher

- Publicist

- Sound Technician

- Stage Manager

Editor's Note: The US Department of Labor's Bureau of Labor Statistics provides information about hundreds of career options. The agency's Occupational Outlook Handbook describes the education and skill requirements, pay, and future outlook for each job. The Occupational Outlook Handbook can be found online at www.bls.gov/ooh.

GLOSSARY

album
a collection of recorded songs

disorder
a condition that affects a person's ability to function

genre
a category or type

internship
a period of training or work that helps someone learn about a certain job

playlist
a collection of various songs by different artists

record
a disc on which a song or collection of songs have been recorded

royalty
payment that songwriters receive each time their songs are played

venue
a place where concerts and events take place

INDEX

IMAGE CREDITS

ABOUT THE AUTHOR

Marty Erickson is a genderqueer writer living in Minnesota. Marty uses the pronouns "they/them/theirs." They write books for young people full time and like to go hiking.